DESIGNER DREAMS
BY LORRAINE SINTETOS

Reading Skills for Life

Level A

Book 2

AGS®

American Guidance Service , Inc.
Circle Pines, Minnesota 55014-1796
1-800-328-2560

Development and editorial services provided by Straight Line Editorial
Development, Inc.

Illustrations: Wendy Cantor

Printed in the United States of America

ISBN 0-7854-2650-7

Product Number 91704

A 0 9 8 7 6 5 4

Contents

1. Girls Like Us

"**K**ate! Thanks to you, I was a smash hit!"

Kate looked up from the sketch she was making. She saw her best friend, Amber, grinning at her.

"What do you mean?" asked Kate.

Amber flopped down on the bed. "Your top made me the glam girl. Lots of people said I looked great, even Jolie Wilson."

"Really? Cool." Kate was acting very calm, but inside she was pleased. Jolie was one of the most stylish girls in school. She always looked very hip, like her stuff was from New York or L.A.

"Are you kidding? It is more than cool." Amber was still smiling.

Kate smiled back. She had made Amber's top. It was red with black trim. Thin black straps crossed in the back and came around to the front. Kate was mad about fashion. Each day she would flip through mags and think about new designs. Most were things she could not make. She could only sketch them. Kate wanted her styles to be cutting edge. She liked to add in surprises, like fringe made out of buttons or fabric that looked like grass.

"So did Jake see you looking hot today?" Kate asked.

Amber sat up as Kim came in.

"What is up with Jake? Are you two going out?" asked Kim.

"No way," said Amber. "He is not for me."

Kim looked at Amber and said, "That is a cute top. I really like that style. I wish I had one like it."

"Kate made it," said Amber.

"If you get me the cloth, I will make you one," said Kate.

Amber asked, "What are you doing now?" She got up and looked at Kate's paper.

Kate had made a new sketch. This style had short black pants and a red tank top with silver ribbon running through it.

"Is that sweet or what?" said Amber.

"I wish I had the big bucks you need to really make things like this," Kate said.

"You will. One day you will be a big name in fashion," Kim told her. "You will have all the cash you need."

"And I will be her model." Amber jumped up on Kim's bed. She put one hand on her hip. She held her other hand out in front of her. "Can you see me on the ramp?"

"Me, too," said Kim. She jumped up on the bed and said, "And here comes the hot model Kim Miller. She has on red silk and . . ."

"What are you girls doing on the bed?" Mrs. Dorn broke in. They had not seen her come in.

Amber and Kim jumped down.

"Not a thing," said Kim.

"You must all have home work to do," said Mrs. Dorn. Then she walked to Kate's bed. She looked at the sketch in Kate's hands. "That is not home work."

"No." Kate did not look at her.

"Kate, you need to stop dreaming and work on your school work. This is your last year in high school. If you keep wasting time with these silly sketches, you will never be able to get a real job."

"What do you mean?" asked Kate.

"You know what I mean. Girls like you do not go to fashion schools. You have to go to the schools that are here in Cactus Bend. You must get skills that will help you get a real job," Mrs. Dorn told them all. "You can work in a bank or look after the sick. You can clean homes or look after people's kids. That is the kind of work you can do. And you will be lucky to get those jobs."

No one said a thing.

"Well, I came to tell you it is time to start dinner." Mrs. Dorn left them.

Girls like them! No one had to ask what Mrs. Dorn was talking about. Girls like them were girls who lived in the Gateway Home. Some had no mom or dad. Some, like Amber, had people who did not want to look after them. Some had people who could not look after them. Kim's mom was sick and lived on the streets. Kate did not know where her mom was. She knew where her dad was—he was doing time. He could not send her to a fashion school. She knew that!

"What ever," said Amber. "You will work in fashion, and I will show off your styles." Amber went back into her pose. "And you must be so very, very rich to have a real Kate Landers dress!"

It was no use. Their game was not fun any more.

2. The Contest

Kate put away the last of Mrs. Yee's clean plates. She wiped the area around the sink. This was her after-school job. Three days a week she helped Mrs. Yee clean. Two times a week, after dinner, she looked after Mrs. Yee's two girls so that Mrs. Yee could teach. Mrs. Yee needed help because she could not walk with out the help of two canes. When she was home, she mostly wheeled herself from place to place.

Kate liked Mrs. Yee. She was always kind and had time to talk. Kate really liked the two little girls, Lily and Rose, even if they were a lot of work. Working there was almost like having a home. She could not remember what having a real home was like. She had lived with her dad and Gran. Dad was never there, so Gran had looked after Kate. Then Gran got sick. She had to go to a home.

Gran never came back. It had been just Dad and Kate for a time. But Dad always had some fishy deal going on. And Kate had landed in Gateway Home.

Kate walked over to Mrs. Yee's desk. "Is there more for me to do?"

"Please sit down, Kate," said Mrs. Yee.

Kate took a seat next to her.

Mrs. Yee went on, "You have looked sad all day. Do you want to tell me about it?"

Kate looked down at her lap. What good could it do to tell Mrs. Yee? But Kate needed to talk to some one. She told Mrs. Yee about her dreams of being a designer. She also told her what Mrs. Dorn had said.

Kate asked, "Is she right? Are girls like me just going to be stuck in Cactus Bend?"

"Right off, we need to talk about the kind of girl you are," Mrs. Yee told her. "I know you by now. You work hard here. You are smart. Your art teacher tells me you do good work. You see things in a fresh way. I believe you have what it takes to do what you want."

Kate shrugged. "But I don't even know how to begin. I read about up and coming designers but I don't know how they got started. Some of them go to top design schools, like the Chicago School of Fashion. But I don't have a rich mom and dad like other kids."

"That does not matter, Kate. Just work on your skills. Ask for help when you need it. And remember it is OK to take risks." Mrs. Yee smiled at her.

Then Kate smiled, too. As she walked home, she was feeling a little better.

The next day, Kate went to Mrs. Yee's after dinner. Mrs. Yee greeted her and waved some pages at Kate. "You will not believe what I have here. We could not ask for better luck!"

"What can she mean?" Kate mused. "And why is she saying 'we'?"

"Come in and sit down," Mrs. Yee told her. "After talking to you, I wanted to know more about design schools. I looked up the Chicago School of Fashion on the Web. It is a very good school. I can see why you want to go there. But that is not my news," she said. "Look at this!"

She held out the pages. Kate could see that this was an application of some kind.

Mrs. Yee went on, "The school is having a contest. The winner gets into the school and does not have to come up with any fees. Plus, the winner gets a free place to live and free meals."

Kate said, "That sounds cool, but I would have to win the contest. And I never win anything. What would I have to do?"

"The rules are here." Mrs. Yee looked at the page. "You must send them ten sketches. You also must send two styles that you made. You can work on those things here and use my Singer."

"When do they want these things?" asked Kate.

"By June 15."

"That is only six weeks away! That is too little time," said Kate.

"Kate! You should not think like that!" Mrs. Yee told her. "If you try, you may or may not win this contest. But if you do not try, then you know you will not win."

"Well, OK. You could be right," said Kate. "I just may do it."

Mrs. Yee handed the application to Kate. "The ball is in your court now."

3. Keeping a Secret

Kate's dreams were filled with fashions of all kinds now—hot pink tops, red belts, black jackets with sparkly hoods. She did not say a word to any one for two days. But by day three, she could not keep the news in.

On their way home from school, she told Amber about the contest.

"You are so going to win!" Amber yelled.

"No, I am not going to win," Kate said. "Things never seem to work out for me. That is why I am asking you not to tell any one."

"Why does it matter?" Amber did not get it.

"If I tell people about the contest," said Kate, "they will think I am bragging that I am going to win it. If you and I keep mum, then no one will know if I do not win."

Then Kate added, "I really do NOT want Mrs. Dorn to know. She will say, 'I told you so.' Then she will say that I do not use my time wisely, and she will give me more jobs to do. If you tell any one, Mrs. Dorn will find out."

"OK," Amber said. She was about to say more when Kate shushed her. A tall girl was walking by them. She gave Kate a mean look as she passed.

"Jess is another one who would give you a hard time," Amber said. "She is one nasty girl. I do not get her."

"Who does?" asked Kate.

Jess did not like any one, but she seemed to like Kate least of all. When Kate had first come to Gateway Home, it had been hard for her to talk to the girls. Jess had hissed at her, "You think you are too good to be here! You think you are better than the rest of us." That had not been so. Kate had just been too upset to speak. Now she was used to the home, and she got along with the other girls. She had even told Jess she would lend her some fashions. But Jess was still full of spite. She put Kate down when she could. She played small, mean tricks on her. Kate did not tell Mrs. Dorn about that stuff. It would not help.

"Well, my lips are zipped," Amber said. "But it will be hard. I will be thinking about it all the time."

Kate did not have much free time, but she worked on her sketches when ever she could. She had to keep up her tasks at Gateway. Plus, she had her job with Mrs. Yee. She also had to make time to do her home work. Mrs. Yee had told her, "You have to keep your grades up. It means that you are some one who can do well if she puts her mind to it."

Kate was surprised to find out that the work did not go very fast. It was one thing to make sketches for fun. It was another thing to make them for the contest. She could not let any mistakes get by. If the sketch did not look right, she started it over.

A week passed. Kate had made only two sketches that she really liked. One day she told Mrs. Yee, "I am trying hard, but I am not sure I can do this. It takes more time than I have."

"You could give up your job here for a week or two," said Mrs. Yee. She looked a little glum.

"Thanks," said Kate. "But I know you really need me. It would be hard to find some one to take my place just now."

Mrs. Yee could not help looking glad. "I will try to think of some thing."

"I will keep on trying," Kate told her. "It is not easy, but I will not give up yet."

The next day, Kate had a surprise in her art class. She was cleaning up her work area. Mr. Bell, the art teacher, said, "Will you see me after class, Kate? I want to talk to you."

What could be the matter? Kate had been working hard in class. She could not think of a thing that he could have to say to her.

When the rest left, Kate went up to Mr. Bell's desk.

He smiled and said, "Mrs. Yee is a friend of mine. She thinks a lot of you."

Kate felt her cheeks get pink.

Mr. Bell went on, "She talked to me about the contest. She said, too, that you are short on time. We came up with a plan. You can do your fashion sketches when you are in art class."

"That would be great! But . . ." Kate stopped. "The kids in the class will know. I had hoped no one would find out about the contest."

"I will tell them that I am letting you work on your job skills. You can tell them what you want."

"Mr. Bell," said Kate, smiling, "you are OK!"

4. The Fabric Search

Kate and Amber were sitting on Kate's bed, looking at two new sketches. Kate had not wanted to leave them at school over the week end.

"This one is really cool!" said Amber. She was looking at a sketch of a short red skirt with a flap that hung down on one side. A wide black and white belt went over it. "Are you going to make this skirt to send in?"

"Could be," said Kate. "I have to see what fabric I can find. Then I will plan it all."

"Where are you going to look for fabric?"

"The only place is the dime store. At times they have OK fabric, but most of the time . . ." Kate made a face. Cactus Bend was not very big, so it did not have many stores. And it was out in the desert. The next city was Red Rock, ten miles away.

Kate went on, "And I am short on cash. I have just nine bucks." Mrs. Dorn gave Kate five bucks a week to spend. She put the rest of what Mrs. Yee gave Kate into the bank. The rest of the girls got five bucks a week, too, from doing more than their share of chores at the home or from having other jobs.

"I can lend you three," said Amber.

"Oh, thanks. It still is not much, is it?" Kate looked at the sketch in her hands. "I just have to make the cash go as far as I can."

After dinner, Kate and Amber walked to the dime store. They went to the back of the store to look at the fabric.

Kate held up some pink fabric. It had pale green leaves. On each leaf was a white bug. She said, "Ick. This stuff is so nasty."

Amber helped Kate look over the fabrics. There was kids' fabric with little fish and some with dogs in hats. There was fabric with big red roses and fabric with small green dots.

"Pretty lame," agreed Amber.

"What am I going to do?" said Kate. "I need some fabric that is stylish and hip. And none of these are any good."

"How about taking the bus to Red Rock?" asked Amber.

"Not a bad idea," said Kate. She checked out a sticker on the fabric. "Man, look at what fabric costs! I just hope I find some on sale."

"Remember bus fare," added Amber.

The girls looked at each other glumly.

"Maybe Mrs. Dorn will let you take some cash out of the bank," said Amber as they walked home.

"Right. And pigs will fly," Kate told her. "Any way, she would ask what I want it for. And I am not going to tell her."

When they got home, it was late. Amber watched TV with the other girls. Kate was trying to sketch, but she was not into it.

As Kate was getting into bed, Amber came in and held up a black bath mat. "How about making a jacket out of this?" she joked. "Fake mink!"

Kate made her self smile. "Right, and I can make a skirt from the drapes. Talk about glam."

It was a while before Kate could go to sleep. But at last she did. She dreamed she was on a ramp at a fashion opening. She had on a jacket made from the black bath mat. The ramp was shaking. She woke up. The ramp was still shaking.

"Kate, wake up!" said Amber. She was shaking Kate. Amber had come in barefoot so that she would not wake up Kim in the other bed.

"Uhhh . . ." muttered Kate. "It is dark out! What do you want?"

"It just came to me—the flea market!"

"What?" Kate was still sleepy.

"You can get what you need at the flea market," Amber said.

"Not really," said Kate. "I have to make the styles my self, not fix up stuff that other people made."

"I know that! But you can cut things up and use the fabric." Amber forgot to whisper.

Kim stirred in her bed.

Kate sat up and smiled. "Amber, smart thinking. We will hit the flea market in the morning. Now let me get some sleep!"

In the morning, while they were all eating, Kim said, "I had a funny dream, Amber. I dreamed that you and Kate were going to the flea market."

"We are," Amber told her.

"Cool," said Kim. "I can read minds in my sleep!"

5. Good Finds and a Bad Surprise

Amber held up a red shirt. "How about this?"

Kate was in the stall across the way. "Not bad, but it is so small. Maybe I could use it for trim." Kate dug through a bunch of tops and held one up. "Check out these sparkly gold buttons! I want to get this."

Kate was digging in her pocket for cash.

"Yo, Kate! Amber!" a boy called out.

Their friend Mike was in the next stall. Kate worked beside him in art class. He was a star athlete, but he was also really good at art.

"Hi! What are you doing here?" asked Amber.

He held up some sneakers. "Just shopping for kicks. I got these for six bucks. Not bad. You looking for any one thing?"

"Looking for things for Kate to make fashions from," Amber told him.

"Right." He had seen Kate's sketches in class and told her they were cool. "Want some help?"

He walked along with them and then fell back when he stopped at a stall full of junk.

"How about this?" asked Mike. "How do I look?"

Kate and Amber turned. Mike had put on a ratty fur jacket and a rubber cat mask.

"You look like what the bus ran over," Kate told him.

They all grinned. Even if Mike did not help much, he made the hunt more fun. When it was time to go home, Kate and Amber had three big bags full of things to cut up.

Kate was stoked now. After dinner, she washed the things she had gotten and hung them up to dry. Later, she would cut them up. Looking at the fabric was giving her ideas. She went to work on a new sketch. She could see the gold buttons hanging off the edge of a skirt.

She was feeling on top of things when she went to her job at Mrs. Yee's on Monday.

"Why the big smile?" asked Mrs. Yee. Kate filled her in on the trip to the flea market.

"What a smart thing to do!" said Mrs. Yee. "Can you use more fabric?"

"Yes. Why?" asked Kate.

"I have some things you can have," Mrs. Yee told her. "Why I did not get rid of them before I will never know. Maybe I was keeping them for you."

Mrs. Yee wheeled down the hall and out into the back yard. She told Kate to look in the shed. "The boxes we want are on the right, I think. They say 'Jean's things.' My mom packed the boxes."

Kate pulled out three big boxes. and opened them. The things in the boxes were really cool.

"Some of that stuff is from the 1960s," said Mrs. Yee. "Like that skirt."

The skirt had big stars and suns in gold, sea green, red, and plum. "The print is hip," said Kate. "I can see this as part of a vest. Maybe I would add some red trim." She pulled out a black shirt with silver dots and some dark red velvet pants. "Cool! What I could do with this fabric!"

"Take what you like," said Mrs. Yee.

When Kate went home that day, she had two more bags of things to use.

She was humming when she got home. She put her bags down beside her bed. Then she got a feeling that things were not right. The papers on her desk were not as she had left them.

Two new sketches had been trashed. Some girl had taken dark pens and messed them up. She had put big hats on the girls' heads and dots on their skirts. One jacket was filled in with zigzags.

Kate turned, and there was Jess, grinning.

"Surprise!" said Jess. "You are not the only one who can think up new fashion trends."

6. Paying for a Mistake

"You freak!" yelled Kate. "That is not funny!"

"Stuck-up jerk!" Jess yelled back.

"Trash!"

The yelling and name-calling did not stop there. Other girls came to see what was going on. Some took Kate's side and yelled, too. Kate had a jacket in her hand, and she flung it at Jess.

No one had seen Mrs. Dorn come up. The jacket hit Mrs. Dorn's arm, but not very hard. "What is this all about?" Mrs. Dorn looked mad.

"I am out of here," said one girl. "Mrs. Dorn is going to go off."

"Jess messed up my sketches!" said Kate.

"Big deal. It was just a little joke." Jess gave Kate a black look.

"It was not a little joke! You are such a . . ."

"They were just lame sketches . . ."

"Girls!" said Mrs. Dorn. "One at a time."

After each one had talked, Mrs. Dorn was still cross. "No one is in the right here. Jess, you know better than to mess with things that are not yours. You know that was not really funny. You will have to make it up to Kate. She will get your five bucks this week so that she can get more paper and pens."

"It is not about the paper and pens," Kate told her.

"And you, Kate, lost your temper over very little. Look at all those sketches." Mrs. Dorn waved her hand at the wall over Kate's bed. "What is one or two more or less?" she said. "The two of you are to blame. You know what happens when you forget the rules. For the next two weeks, you can leave here only to go to school."

"But what about my job for Mrs. Yee?" asked Kate. "She really does need me."

"All right." Mrs. Dorn nodded. "Go to your job. But you had better not stop on the way there or back."

"I bet she will stop," Jess said crossly. "No one will know if she does."

"You will know," said Mrs. Dorn. "I want you to walk her to her job and back. Because you two are so fond of each other, I think you need to spend more time with one another."

"No!" said both girls at the same time.

"Yes," said Mrs. Dorn, "and I do not want to have to talk to you another time."

Kate was not upset about going only to school and to her job. She had lots to do at home for the contest. She was just upset about the messed up sketches.

"Right now," Kate told Mrs. Yee a day later, "I just want to give up. I put so much work into sketches, and now I have to start over."

"I am not surprised that you feel that way," said Mrs. Yee. "It was a very mean thing for Jess to have done. I wonder why she did it."

"Because she is a pig," said Kate.

"Come on, Kate."

Kate looked away. She did not want Mrs. Yee to think less of her. "I am just going to forget the contest. It will take too long to do those sketches over."

"I find that hard to believe. You would let a little thing like this stop you?" asked Mrs. Yee. "That is not like you, Kate."

Kate turned pink. "Well, no."

"So?" asked Mrs. Yee.

"OK. I will do the sketches over," said Kate. Then she smiled. "You know, I bet I can make them even better."

"Great," said Mrs. Yee. "I have set up the Singer for you. You can work on the fashions while you look after Lily and Rose. I have to get going, or I will be late."

The little girls were good and hardly fussed at all. After Kate read to them, they went right to sleep. Kate was surprised at how much work she did. She was feeling fine by the time Mrs. Yee came home.

The good feeling went away when she reached the gate. There was Jess with a grim look on her face. Jess turned away and took such big steps that Kate had to rush to keep up with her. No one said a thing all the way home.

7. Another Surprise From Jess

Kate sat on Mrs. Yee's rug, pinning the parts of a top. Mrs. Yee had gone out to teach, and the girls were feeling spunky. Kate had read to them for a long time, but they wanted more from her.

"Play with us!" Rose tugged at Kate's arm.

"Look out for that pin! Come on. You know lots of games the two of you can play." Kate wanted to get on with her work.

Lily yelled, "No!"

"You tell us a game," Rose said.

"Tell you a game . . ." It was hard to think of one. Kate spotted a box in the hall. It was one of the ones that said 'Jean's things.' Kate got up and pushed the box on to the rug. It was so big that it could hold both girls.

"Go and get the stuff you wore to trick-or-treat," Kate said.

"What are we going to play?" asked Rose.

"A new game," Kate said.

The girls ran out and came back with their stuff. They and a friend had been the Three Little Pigs. Kate helped them get on pink PJs. She put a hood with floppy ears on each one.

"There," she said. "Now you are dressed to go off in space. See that box? It is really a space ship."

Rose stamped one foot. "There are no little pigs in space!"

"Did I say you were little pigs?" asked Kate. "No, what you are is big bad space hogs from Mars."

"I am a big, bad space hog," sang Lily. The girls got into the box. They made the sounds of space guns. "We are going as fast as mom's car," Rose told Lily. "We may run into the sun!"

The girls were happy out in space. Plus, Kate got a lot of work done on her top. She was hemming it when Mrs. Yee came home. She held it up to show Mrs. Yee.

"Very nice," said Mrs. Yee.

Rose ran up, gripping her pink rabbit by one leg. "Mom, we had to blast Mr. Bun! He was going to take over Mars."

"Then it is a good thing you blasted him," agreed Mrs. Yee.

"I let the girls play," Kate told her. "They were too full of pep to go to bed."

Mrs. Yee said, "I can see that. It is OK. I am glad to see them having so much fun. You are very good with kids, Kate."

"It is not all me. They are good kids," said Kate. Still, what Mrs. Yee said made her feel great.

She walked out of Mrs. Yee's home smiling. Not even Jess could wreck that fine feeling.

Jess was swinging on the gate. "I could see in. Did you make that top?"

Kate nodded.

"I bet I could make one just as good," said Jess.

"May be you could." Kate did not think about what Jess said. She did not feel like having a spat.

It was getting dark. A little dog ran out on to the walk and yapped at them.

"Chill out, boy," said Jess.

The dog trotted in front of them. Right then, a bike whizzed by. The dog ran out to bark at it. The front wheel of the bike clipped the dog, but the rider did not stop.

Jess yelled, "You scum!"

The dog was on its side, yelping. Kate did not know what to do. How could she help the dog? Would it bite her if she got close to it?

Jess did not stop to think. She fell down on her knees by the dog. "Good boy," she said. "It will be all right. That's a good boy." The dog stopped

31

yelping. She ran her hands all over him. He licked one hand. "I think he is just winded. He came out of that yard. Go see if the people who live there are home. Tell them their dog needs to see a vet."

Kate did as Jess said. A woman was home and rushed out. The girls helped her put the dog in her van so that the woman could take him to a vet. It was really Jess who did the helping.

"That was great," said Kate after the van went away. "You are good with dogs."

"No," said Jess as she shrugged. "I am not good at any thing. That is what people have been saying for years."

"That is such trash!" Kate told her. "You did just the right thing. I bet you could be a vet."

"Could be." It was dark then, but Kate saw Jess smile just a little.

8. Gone!

In no time at all, it was the day before the application and fashions had to be shipped.

Kate and Amber still had not told any one about the contest. The other girls believed that Kate was just making new styles for fun.

There was no more work to do on the ten sketches, and Kate had filled out the application. But there was still some work to do on the styles. Two tops needed to be hemmed. A jacket needed buttons. Kate had them at home with her now, so she could work on them.

Kim sat on the next bed. She held a top up in front of her. "This is so me! Will you lend it to me?"

"OK," said Kate. "But not now. I have other plans for it right now."

"Do you have a date?" Another girl had come into the room.

"What do you need to know for?" Kate grinned. "There! That is the last button on this jacket."

Jess had come in, too. Jess did not seem like the same girl now. Kate had told all the girls how good Jess had been with the dog. They had been much better to Jess and agreed that she could be a vet if she wanted to. Jess was not as hard to be around, and she smiled more.

Jess picked a vest up off the bed. It was the one Kate had made from Mrs. Yee's skirt. "I bet this fits me."

"Try it on," said Kate.

Jess put on the vest.

"Hot!" said Kim.

"You go around in that, and you got game!" said another girl.

"I will lend it to you," Kate told Jess. "One day."

It was a while before Jess took the vest off. Kate could see that Jess really liked it.

After dinner, Kate and Amber sat on Kate's bed. They were the only ones there.

"What is your plan now?" asked Amber.

Kate held up a top. "I have to hem this, and then I am through. I still need to get a big box. After school, I can pick one up at the drug store. Then I pack my things and take the box to UPS. They shut down at five, so I will have plenty of time."

Amber looked at the fashions that were hanging up. "You are in the zone! I think you will win the contest."

"Look, a lot of people will send in good work. It is hard to believe that mine will stand out." Kate put her hand on Amber's arm. "Thanks for not telling the others. I feel a little sick—and freaked out—right now."

"Just ship the box and forget about it," Amber told her. "What happens, happens."

It was hard for Kate to go to sleep that night, and when day came, it was hard to get up. She was still a little sick. At school, she could not think about her work. In art class, her hands were shaking. It seemed like a very long day, but at last classes were over.

She and Amber stopped at the drug store on the way home and got a box.

"I hope no one is home," said Kate as they walked. "If they see me packing up my styles, they will want to know why."

"Remember, there is a basketball game after school," said Amber. "Most of the girls were planning to go."

Kate and Amber went up the steps of Gateway. Amber went in before Kate. "Come on. No one is around."

Kate rushed down the hall with the box and then dropped it on her bed. "All right! We got in with out being seen! Now we have to pack up and get out. Fast." Kate put her sketches in the box. She took down a top. She wrapped it in paper and put it in the box.

Then Amber handed her a skirt. With Amber's help, the packing went fast.

Kate was about to put the application into the box. "Hold it." She stopped to think. She looked over the things in the box. Her face turned white.

Amber said, "What is it, Kate? You look as if you saw a ghost!"

"Amber, do you remember giving me the vest with the star print?"

Amber stopped to think, too. "No . . ."

"Where is it, then? One of the girls must have it!"

9. On the Track of the Missing Vest

"Just a sec," said Amber. "May be it is still here."

They looked all around. Amber even looked under the beds. But they did not spot the vest.

They raced into the hall and ran into Kim eating a snack. Kim told them that she had not seen the vest.

"Are you the only one here?" asked Kate.

"Yes. The rest went to the basketball game." Kim made a face. "Basketball is not my thing."

"I have to get to that game!" Kate rushed down the hall. "I bet one of them has my vest."

It was ten blocks to the school. Kate and Amber ran each step of the way.

The sound of kids yelling came from in back of the school where the basketball court was. The two girls raced around the school and to the court. Kate looked at the people in the bleachers but did not see any of the girls from Gateway.

"Look over there," called Amber. "I see Kelly! And I see Jess in your vest!"

Kate could see Jess, too, because Jess was on her feet, yelling.

The fans were yelling for Kate's friend Mike. He was standing on a line, about to take a free shot at a basket. He would shoot the basket and score.

Kate did not seem to see Mike or the basketball game. All she could see was Jess in the missing vest. Kate rushed right on to the basketball court. The players just looked on in surprise. Mike dropped the ball.

Kate rushed up the bleachers to where Jess was. "Give me that vest!"

The coach ran across the court. "You nuts?"

Jess looked from Kate to the coach. She hopped off the bleachers and ran behind the school. Kate ran after Jess, the coach ran after Kate, and Amber ran after all of them.

"Come back here!" yelled the coach.

They ran with out stopping. The coach gave up and went back to the court. After all, the game was not over.

The girls ran past the school and on and on. At last, at the park, Jess could run no more. She fell to her knees on the grass under a tree.

"My vest," Kate panted. "I want my vest."

Jess slipped the vest off and gave it to her.

"What is the big deal? You said you would lend it to me."

"But not now." Kate could not say another thing.

Amber flopped down on the grass, too.

Kate had the vest on her lap. She was shaking her head. "It is over. I am sure it is close to five. UPS will close before I get there."

"What is this all about?" asked Jess.

"I better tell her," said Amber. She filled Jess in about the contest. ". . . And this is the last day to send the things in."

"You should have told us," said Jess. "If you had told us, I never . . ."

"Forget it." Kate looked into space.

"Kate thinks she may not win," Amber said, "so she made me keep it a secret."

"So she does not win. So what?" said Jess. "As long as she gave it a try."

Kate looked at Jess in surprise. Even Jess seemed a little surprised by what she had said.

"We better jam," said Amber. "It is about time to fix dinner."

They got to their feet and walked home.

Kate put the vest on her bed. She could not take the things out of the box. Not yet. She went to help with dinner.

Jess left them and went down the hall. In a short time, she came back, looking pleased. "I called UPS. They close at six in Red Rock. My friend Jim will lend me his car. You pack up the box, and I will take it to Red Rock."

Kate's face lit up. Then she looked at the clock. "Thanks, Jess. But you would have to really speed to make it on time. You could get killed. I have to say no."

"You care if I get killed?" asked Jess.

"Yes, you dimwit."

"I am really sorry about the vest," Jess said.

"No big deal," Kate said. "I will live."

10. Not Over Yet

After dinner, Kate pushed the box behind her desk. She flopped on her bed and looked at the wall.

Jess came in and sat down on Kim's bed. She picked at Kim's blanket but did not speak.

Then Amber came in and sat next to Jess. "Giving up now is just silly."

"I have to. The rules said the things had to be shipped by this date." Kate did not look up.

"People can bend rules," Amber said. "UPS is open on week ends. You can still ship the box. Just send it and put in a letter that tells what happened."

"It was my bad," said Jess. "I am not a great writer, but I will write, too, and tell them how I messed you up."

Kate sat up and felt a rush of hope. "OK, why not? I will just try."

The girls helped Kate wrap the vest and seal the box after the letters went into it.

"I will get Jim's car in the morning and drive you there," said Jess.

They all felt better now. Kate said, "Well, this is a day I will never forget."

"You know what I will never forget?" put in Jess. "The look on the coach's face when you ran on to the court."

"Oh, man!" Amber grinned.

Kate could not help but grin, too.

Then Amber and Jess snickered. Soon they all could not hold back.

Kim came in. "Do you want to let me in on the big joke?"

A week went by, then two weeks. Then three weeks had passed.

Kate told herself, "I will not think about the contest. I will forget about it. What happens, happens." Both Amber and Jess had said that they would still keep their lips zipped.

One day when they were fixing dinner, Jess rushed in looking really happy. "Get this! I got a part-time job."

"For real? Doing what?" one girl asked.

"Working for the vet. They want me to clean up and help care for the pets that have to spend some time there."

Kate asked, "How did you get the job? Was it in the paper?"

"No. I just went in and asked if they needed

help. I said to myself, 'I will just have to try.' " Jess looked thrilled.

"Right on!" Kate said.

Mrs. Dorn was there, too, and said, "Jess, you did just great! I will cut back on some of your chores here so you have time for your new job."

Kate was glad for Jess. Hard as it was to believe, she had come to think of Jess as a friend.

Jess's good news made Kate wish she had her own news one way or the other. At last she broke down and talked to Amber about the contest. "I keep thinking that it was not OK to ship the box late. There is no way I can win."

"Cut it out, Kate," Amber told her. "They still have the box. That proves they are looking at your fashions. They would have sent it back if you were out of the contest."

"Right," Kate said dully. She did not seem to believe Amber.

When they got home that day, Mrs. Dorn stopped them in the hall. "Kate, a big box came for you today. I put it on your bed."

Kate's face turned pale. In a flat tone, she said, "Well, they did send the box back. So what does that prove?"

11. What Happens, Happens

The box sat on the rug by Kate's bed. She would not go close to it. She sat at dinner with out speaking.

"What is the matter with her?" Jess asked Amber.

Amber leaned close to Jess. "The box came back."

"So?" Jess looked at Kate. "What was in it?"

"Who knows?" said Amber. "She would not even open it."

Kate knew what they were saying. "What is in it? Just what I put in it. No surprises. Forget it, OK?"

The other two girls would not let her forget it. After dinner, they did the dishes and then tagged after Kate. She sat down at her desk and got out her home work. They went to stand next to her.

"Can you believe her?" Jess asked Amber. Then she said to Kate, "You think there are snakes in there?"

"Open the box," Amber told Jess. "I bet they sent a nice letter."

"So what?" Kate did not look up from her work.

With Amber's help, Jess got the box open.

"Look! They did send a letter." Amber reached for it.

"And . . .?" asked Jess.

Kate stopped reading but did not turn around.

Amber held up the letter. "It says: Dear Ms. Jackson. Thank you for letting us see your fine work."

"See. They said, 'fine work,'" Jess told Kate.

Amber read on, "We wish that there could be more than one winner of our contest. We are sorry to say that you did not win but . . ."

"Big surprise," Kate said flatly.

"Shut up! There is more." Amber read, "Even so, we would be happy to have you at our school. We can not give you your living costs, but we would take care of your school fees if you come in the fall. We hope that you will write back to say . . ."

"They want me!" Kate yelled.

"We told you you were good!" Amber hugged her.

Three other girls ran in to see what the yelling was about. Amber told them all about the contest. Kate was too stunned to speak. She just read the letter over and over.

Then Mrs. Dorn came in and asked, "What is all this racket?"

"Can you believe it! Kate won a fashion contest!" said one of the girls.

Then Amber told Mrs. Dorn all about it, too.

Mrs. Dorn asked to see the letter. She read it over. "Well, this is a real surprise. I did not know you were that good, Kate."

Kate could speak now. "I was not the real winner. All they said was that they would take care of my fees, not my living costs. What I have in the bank is way less than what I would need to live on my own." She smiled. "But may be I can keep saving and go there the year after. I will write to them and ask them if they will hold a place for me. You know, I am OK with that. It just feels so great to know that they think I could be a designer."

"Well, good for you, Kate," said Mrs. Dorn. "May be I was wrong to think that you did not have the skills or the drive to find a job in fashion. I am glad to be wrong about some things," she said as she walked out.

"I must call Mrs. Yee," Kate said, but the other girls would not let her go. They made her take all

47

her things out of the box. Some wanted to take turns trying on the fashions.

"Now I will lend you that top," Kate told Kim.

"Kate!" Mrs. Dorn had come back. "Kate, I would like to talk to you for a little while."

Kate went out into the hall with Mrs. Dorn. She could not think why Mrs. Dorn wanted to talk to her. Mrs. Dorn had already said she had been wrong—right in front of the other girls.

"Kate, you proved that you can go after what you want and work hard to get it. The letter tells me that you have the skills to do it. I was down on you before because I really believed you were just dreaming. I wanted you to make wiser plans than that." Mrs. Dorn looked at her with more kindness than Kate had seen before. "I came here to tell you that you can go to that school this fall if you want."

"Are you kidding? How?" Kate gasped.

"Mrs. Yee told me how good you are with kids. My sister lives in Chicago. She has a little boy and will have a little girl in the fall. I called her just now. You can stay at her home for free if you help out with the kids and the chores." Now Mrs. Dorn was really smiling.

"Mrs. Dorn," said Kate, "now I do feel as if I must be dreaming."